Outsmart Your Brain

Identify and Control Unconscious Judgments,
Protect Yourself From Exploitation, and Make
Better Decisions

The Psychology of Bias, Distortion and
Irrationality

Steven Schuster

understanding that the author is not engaged in rendering medical, legal or other professional advice or services. If professional assistance is required, the services of a competent professional person should be sought. The author shall not be liable for damages arising herefrom. The fact that an individual, organization of website is referred to in this work as a citation and/or potential source of further information does not mean that the author endorses the information the individual, organization to website may provide or recommendations they/it may make. Further, readers should be aware that Internet websites listed in this work might have changed or disappeared between when this work was written and when it is read.

For general information on the products and services or to obtain technical support, please contact the author.

Table of Contents

Introduction

Think about the last time you made a decision. Was it to call your mother? Or perhaps to wait for the express train to come instead of the local, or to go through the yellow light instead of stopping? We all make thousands of these small decisions every day, and most of the time they prove to be correct. If you did not get in a car accident when you decided to go through the yellow light or made better time to work by taking the express, this was probably the right choice. Humans are generally good decision-makers; otherwise, we would be getting into accidents and making people angry all the time, and it would be a struggle to get through daily life.

We all also make more difficult decisions: which job offer to take, whether to make an offer on a house or apartment, whether to invest our money in the stock market or put it in a retirement account. Economists have assumed for years that people make all these decisions rationally, meaning that they will think about the pros and cons of each choice, project future consequences, and then make an educated decision based on this thought process. This assumption has allowed economists to create many different models that excel at predicting large-scale events like stock market fluctuations, recessions, voting patterns, and consumer actions.

However, these models do not work to describe every kind of behavior. Sometimes people don't act according to what economists believe are rational choices. They don't always spend more money when there's a sale, or they end up ordering their old standby meal because a restaurant menu has *too many* options. As the field has developed in the last fifty years, decision scientists have created a new field called behavioral economics that combines psychology, economics, and neuroscience to better describe decision-making processes in the real world.

This book will serve as an overview of this new field of study.

- The first chapter will be an overview of the basics of what behavioral economics is.
- The second chapter will explore reference dependence, which is one of behavioral economics' fundamental principles.
- The third chapter will detail the implications of reference dependence.
- The fourth chapter will discuss the elements of probability weighting, or how probabilities turn into influences on our decision-making.

- Chapter 5 will deal with risk as it appears in economics, that is, as a decision-making factor.
- Chapter 6 examines the science of comparison.
- Chapter 7 explains the principle of bounded rationality—that is, the inherent limits on rationality in our thinking process.
- Finally, Chapter 8 will discuss how all these principles interact to create models for our social decisions.

This book presents this information with the aim of improving your own decision-making process as you move through life. Although no one can be a perfect decision maker—all people have biases, after all—understanding the process will help you work with these biases and make more informed, well-considered choices that take into account rewards, pain, loss, and risk and provide the most successful results possible.

Chapter 1: What is Behavioral Economics?

As we have already mentioned, behavioral economics combines psychology, economics, and neuroscience to predict and describe decision-making behaviors. There were two problems that drove the creation of the field: whether the underlying principles of economics, utility, and profit are actual drivers of human behavior, and whether people always work to maximize the utility they gain from their decisions. "Utility" here approximately means "benefits;" mostly, it works to expand the parameters of economic behavior from just money and labor to things like time and pleasure.[i]

The ideal person, at least according to an economist, would always make decisions that will result in them gaining the most utility. This "ideal" is called rational choice theory, which is defined as the theory that people will always make the choice that maximizes their own individual satisfaction when given different options under scarcity. "Scarcity" here means that there is a limited quantity of goods—which, since we live on a planet with finite resources, is always true in real life. The best choices, which are the ones that lead to the best outcomes, should therefore come from a prediction of which choice would provide the best utility. The ideal rational decision maker would be so consistent in being able to carry out this process that we would be able to create a mathematical model that successfully predicts their decisions based on utility. This would entail a complete lack of emotions, biases, or external influences. Of course, no person like this actually exists, which is where behavioral economics comes in.

The science of behavioral economics has become particularly relevant in recent years, in the aftermath of the global recession. Many people were left to deal with the weight of their non-rational decisions to buy a home they could not afford, to buy new cars and clothes instead of save for retirement, or even to spend $5 every day on coffee instead of making it at home. This led to widespread struggle that the global economy has still not fully recovered from. Behavioral economics is meant to explain why people made those choices, and what can be done so they make better-considered ones in the future. Its key pioneers are Gary Becker, Herbert Simon, Daniel Kahneman, and George Akerlof, all of whom study or studied human behaviors considered by economists to be irrational.

The people who chose to buy a new car with their bonus instead of pay off credit card debt or save for retirement made decisions that were not in their own self-interest, because people are emotional and biased. Saving for retirement might be more prudent, but retirement seems like an abstract thing far in the future, and advertisements tell us that a new car will make us happy *now*. Although retirement might have crossed people's minds, they wanted a new Mercedes more than being able to afford a nice assisted living facility, which is hard to imagine in the moment. Behavioral economics explains this phenomenon by taking into account influences like advertising, peer pressure, and culture, and how they create cognitive biases that hamper rational decision-making.

What *is* rational decision-making? People often conflate the way we use "rational" in conversation with the way behavioral economists view it; when we use it, we mean someone is logical, in control of their emotions, and thinks through their actions. However, "rational" decisions in economics are decisions that are *consistent* with a model. They don't have to be logically reached or in someone's best self-interest, but they do have to be consistent. This means that a rational decision-maker would always pick the better outcome over the worse one by predicting the amount of utility they would get from each possible outcome. Inconsistency in choices, meanwhile, would disqualify someone from being a rational decision-maker.

Rational decision-makers aren't supposed to be Gordon Gekko-like people who always act selfishly and live by the motto "Greed is good." People who volunteer or make charitable contributions or join the military can still be described with economic models, as long as they derive utility from their choices. It is also important to emphasize that the word "rational" does not refer to the process of decision-making itself, but instead to the results of decisions that provide the most utility, which would be the end result of a rational actor's choices. Rational choice models all tend to be based on consistent, mathematically described decision-making processes, the idea that people always prefer the better option, and that people take actions to get what they prefer to maximize their utility.

Rational choice models are very simple by design. They rely on the principle that people *want* more money. However, if this is incorrect, rational choice models tend to fall apart. For example, economists tend to think that money always works as an incentive. However, this is not always true; sometimes, it can actually *disincentivize* people. Economists call this "reward undermining." This disrupts rational choice models, and we will explore why later in this book. Monetary incentives, like giving employees who work out 50 times in six months a cash bonus, tend to work. However, monetary disincentives happen when money undermines things like moral incentives or happiness. These instances represent failures in rational choice models, but they are not random, rare, or anomalies. They are the result of very specific behavior, which has its roots in psychology, environments, and cognitive science. This is why behavioral economics studies those fields in conjunction with economics.

Rational choice theory tends to be constrained by very specific sets of circumstances dictated by the aforementioned factors. While saving for retirement, refinancing a mortgage, or saving for college can all seem like objectively rational choices, people's biases can lead them away from the choices economists expect them to make. Brains evolved to help make choices related to short-term survival, like when to go out to hunt and when to start storing food, but not relatively modern things like long-term financial planning. This means that brains tend to evaluate information on relative terms, by comparing it to what they already know. This is why, for example, people's happiness tends not to increase with wealth once they are making over $75,000; after this point, instead of being happy that they are making a comfortable living, people compare themselves to those who have even more money, no matter how much money they themselves make. Although it produces interesting psychological quirks like this one, relative processing helps our brains simplify their decision-making. The problem is when the reference point is the incorrect one, giving us skewed perspectives on our circumstances.[ii]

Our brains are also limited because we have limited time to make decisions. Collecting information takes a while, and people cannot always wait to have all the relevant data. For example, looking for an apartment or home can be challenging in a seller's market, because properties move quickly and decisions must be made before necessarily doing a full evaluation of pros and cons for each option. Both of the aforementioned problems can prevent people's decision-making from fitting into economic models.

There are ways to work around these limitations, however. Herbert Simon, an economist and psychologist, invented the theory of bounded rationality, or the idea that rationality can be limited. We can compensate for this with strategies, simplification, and the correct information to make a decision. This does not mean becoming more rigid in adhering to logical processes, or taking longer to reach decisions. It means adopting rules, or heuristics, to select the relevant pieces of information, simplify decisions that are complicated, and applying strategies that require little effort or time. In other words, they're mental strategies to help quicken the decision-making process. These heuristics are just one concept introduced by behavioral economics, and are ideal for practical use in everyday life.[iii]

However, these are not perfect; if a decision made using heuristics is in error, they can also lead to cognitive bias. Behavioral economics has tried to adapt to these biases with behavioral game theory, which is exactly what it sounds like. Game theory is a larger economic theory that helps predict people's choices as influenced by their *own* predictions of other people's behavior. Behavioral game theory applies this to people's irrational choices and why they make them by using external factors, like projections of other people's actions. Behavioral finance is another application, which seeks to describe what drives investors to make irrational choices in markets.

Corporations use behavioral economics principles in their own strategies to generate profit. For example, Apple did a back-to-school sale in the summer of 2019 where customers could get the new Beats wireless headphones with their purchase of a new MacBook. When these headphones were first introduced, they cost around $250, and the computer cost $1100-$2000. If this deal had been introduced when both products came out, people might have still thought the purchase to be too expensive to be worth it. However, knowing the more expensive initial cost for both products, people were now more likely to see the promotion as a deal, and Apple sold more laptops while demand for the Beats headphones increased due to their greater visibility. This is an example of irrational behavioral patterns being weaponized to move more inventory, thanks to a clever application of behavioral economics principles.[iv][1]

---

[1] Disclosure: I'm not affiliated with Apple in any

---

way. I used their promotion to prove my point through a relevant example.

Chapter 2: Reference Dependence

Reference dependence is one of the core principles of behavioral economics. It was developed by Daniel Kahneman and Amos Tversky in their work on prospect theory, which deals with the "reference points" mentioned in the last chapter and how people classify their outcomes based on them. Prospect theory helps explain other human behavioral phenomena, such as loss avoidance. As you might guess, therefore, reference dependence is a widely applicable concept; it can apply to anything related to risk evaluation in decision-making. People tend to make choices about what to do based on what they already know, and their decisions can vary even if the circumstances are exactly the same. For example, although two different people could come to the edge of a crosswalk at the exact same time while the "don't walk" sign is flashing, one person might decide to go for it and cross because of their prior knowledge of how fast they can make it, while the other person might not because of their knowledge that they cannot move fast enough. The two people made different choices because of their different reference points.[v]

It's fairly easy to intuit that different people have different priorities, and that these differences influence decision-making. It might be intuitive that people base the value they anticipate on pleasure both prior and possible, but our brains aren't actually wired for this to be the priority. Instead, our dopamine receptors are actually linked to our brain's reward center. We thus respond to our brain's information about rewards that have happened and could still happen. We can think of value as the information our brains process about our experience and perception of rewards.

This evaluation of reward goes into every decision we make. Think about making a decision whether to take public transportation or a car to work. This will depend on which option you usually choose, what you know about traffic that morning, how comfortable and convenient you find each option, and possibly even the image you want to project as a commuter. All these factors come with what you sense as *value*. This sense of value is what guides all human decision-making. Therefore, if we can calculate and determine value, we can predict every decision a person makes, and why they make them. We can even gain insight into the results of these decisions.

Value comes from both the pleasure and the benefits we experience from any given situation or good. Sometimes these are obvious—

things like food and sleep are necessary for our survival, and make us feel good. Our friends also make us feel good and provide us with a support system. Scientists have even extrapolated this principle to evolution, in a theory called adaptive fitness wherein value corresponds to the degree to which a choice will help someone pass on their genes and continue the species. While all these factors are components of value, however, they don't tell the whole story. Junk food is less nutritious than whole foods, has a negative effect on our health, and might even have side effects that reduce our confidence, such as acne. However, we still choose it over healthy food because it has value in terms of pleasure and deliciousness, which outweighs the benefits. Pleasure and benefit work against each other in this case, and they often do in real life. People buy designer clothes not because they are sturdy or practical, but because they are beautiful; their beauty outweighs their cost. In fact, this is why people often have problems like shopping addictions; they derive value from things other than financial and practical benefits.[vi]

Earlier in this chapter, we mentioned dopamine as a factor in how we experience pleasure and value. Dopamine is a chemical that plays an integral role in how our brains function. Neurons in the brain carry electrical signals to each other; dopamine neurons are a specific subtype of these cells. Every time these neurons send an electrical signal, the signal travels to the synapse, or the gap between neurons, which then signals to release dopamine. Dopamine interacts with the surrounding neurons, making them fire fast and therefore making us feel better. This is where the neuroscience component of behavioral economics comes in; it has recently been discovered that dopamine is a key part of how our brains decide what value is.

You've probably heard of Pavlovian conditioning, or Pavlovian reactions. These popular phrases are based on Ivan Pavlov's well-known neuropsychological experiments on dogs, where he would trigger a salivating response to the sound of a bell by providing food after the bell. Because the dogs learned to expect food after the bell, after extensive conditioning they would salivate at the sound of a bell even if no food followed it. Pavlov believed that this was because the dogs' brains constructed neurons that specifically triggered the salivary response when they received the auditory signals associated with a bell.

Psychologists frequently refer to this experiment in ideas about how past experiences guide human behavior. This phenomenon is called "classical conditioning." Classical conditioning has even been described by a mathematical iterative equation for the probability of the conditioned reaction developed by Robert R. Bush and Frederick Mosteller (though it is often misattributed to Rescorla and Wagner). Basically, the impact of a reward in classical conditioning can be measured based on the reward impact of the previous trial and the learning rate, giving how fast a reward is conditioned into behavior. Rewards also tend to have more of an impact the more recently they occurred. Because this equation uses math to find a quantitative average of past rewards' effects, this is the basis for a more modern understanding of classical conditioning.[vii]

This mathematical model makes conditioning applicable beyond psychology and neuroscience to fields like computer programming and economics. If you take a probability of 0.5 that a reward will happen, for example, and each reward has the same numerical value (let's just call it "6"), then it is easy to plug those values into the equation $R_{next} = R_{previous} + a$(Number of reward opportunities [which is 6 here] – $R_{previous}$). Thus we can put a quantitative value on reward-based conditioning, which is called "expected value" as opposed to the "learning value" a. This number can fit into larger equations to predict behavior, which helps with data processing and behavioral prediction.

The neuroscientist Wolfram Schulz also expanded on Pavlov's work in the early 1990s in monkey experiments designed to test VTA (short for ventral tegmental area, which is a specific neuron group in the brain) dopamine neurons. He found that while the monkeys' dopamine neurons increased their signals when the monkeys were either given juice or given the trigger signal for juice, they actually *decreased* their signals when the monkeys didn't get the expected juice after the trigger signal. He concluded that dopamine neurons are actually activated when our expectations match our reality, and their activity decreases when reality *doesn't* meet expectations. Our dopamine neurons fire the most when we receive an unexpected good thing, and fire the least when the opposite happens—when we expect something good that never comes.[viii]

This study teaches us an important thing: although the popular conception of dopamine is that it is the chemical in the brain that gives us pleasure, it actually correlates more with expectations of pleasure. This is borne out in a study conducted by a team led by the psychologist Kent Berridge. The team knew that rats, like people, make certain expressions associated with pleasure or disgust. So, they decided to use these expressions as their metric for testing rats' dopamine function. They then gave the rats they tested a neurotoxin that targeted neurons in the rats' dopamine systems. Once these neurons were damaged, the researchers found that the rats wouldn't make an effort to get food or juice, no matter how hungry or thirsty they were, because they no longer desired these rewards. However, the rats still ingested food and juice that was placed into their mouths. Furthermore, they still exhibited pleasure expressions when they ingested sugar water, just like normal rats, and also exhibited typical disgust behaviors when they were given lithium water, which is bitter. Therefore, the systems affected by the disabling of the rats' dopamine systems seemed to be connected to motivation for getting a reward, instead of pleasure and displeasure themselves. In other words, the rats no longer *wanted* things. Researchers have found in recent years that the neurons connected to pleasure itself are actually those that use opioids to send electrical signals, but this research is ongoing. The point is, dopamine is connected more to our expectations and desires than to actual events and outcomes.[ix]

A final study that has shed light on the
nature of dopamine is one involving people with
Parkinson's disease. When someone is afflicted
with Parkinson's disease, their dopamine neurons
die out to the point that neurological effects like
loss of balance, diminished motor skills, and
tremors develop. One of the key treatments for
Parkinson's today is actually replenishing the
brain's dopamine and intensifying dopamine's
effects with pharmaceutical drugs. An interesting
topic of study in Parkinson's research is
pathological gambling and other disorders related
to reduced impulse control, which was first
discovered by neurologists in the early 1990s.
Although these early cases didn't attract attention
because it was still thought that Parkinson's was
purely a motor function disorder and was not
related to dopamine or the brain's reward centers.

Parkinson's patients underreport
pathological gambling to doctors and caregivers

(they often result in behaviors frowned upon by society, after all) but rates are significantly higher—2.2 to 7.7%—than those reported in the general population, which has a rate of approximately 1.4% for point occurrence and 5.1% for lifetime occurrence. Impulse control problems tend to be more prevalent among patients who developed the disease earlier in life, or those who already exhibited high-risk behaviors like substance abuse. The high prevalence among Parkinson's patients is thought to be due to the dopamine treatments patients receive in the form of drugs called dopamine agonists, which cause brain chemistry to change and favor impulsive behavior.[x]

These brain chemistry changes were discovered in 2003 by a team from the Muhammad Ali Parkinson's Research Center, which found that the increased dopamine levels used in treatment led to increases in pathological gambling behaviors. Since then, this treatment methodology has continued to be used, but doctors now warn patients about the risk for impulse control problems. These problems have been addressed in more depth in an article published in 2013 by a team from the University of Naples. The authors concluded that increased screening by doctors and caregivers and the development of diagnostics to perform this screening should be priorities in the development of Parkinson's care. They also suggest further investigation into cognitive correlations with pathological gambling in Parkinson's patients, and more research into the genetics of the co-pathologies. Both of these factors could contribute to the reason why some Parkinson's patients develop gambling addictions and others do not.[xi]

So far, the team has reached the same possible options for treatment as previously practiced; that is, tapering off the dopamine supplements to either lower them to the point where behaviors stop, or discontinuing them completely. They also suggest possible other treatments like reducing levodopa (a dopamine replacement), using "atypical antipsychotics," or deep brain stimulation. They ultimately conclude that while pathological gambling can be a side effect of Parkinson's treatments with dopamine agonists, there are other factors that create this psychopathology in both Parkinson's patients and the population as a whole. They believe that these factors can be isolated by finding subtypes of Parkinson's, which could help determine secondary cognitive, neurobiological, or genetic factors that interact with Parkinson's to cause symptoms of pathological gambling.

Dopamine is a powerful chemical; it can even create impulsive behaviors in people who chase the feeling of their receptors lighting up. However, it does not function in as simple a way as we believe. Instead of being purely related to pleasure, it is more dependent on whether our expectations of future pleasure and future value are validated. In this way, dopamine is central to behavioral economics. Reference dependence is all about generating expectations about the value of outcomes based on prior experience; in other words, it is about the conditions that determine whether or not dopamine is released. As Bush and Mosteller proved, the release of dopamine mathematically corresponds to what we conceive of as value. Therefore, we can think of value in behavioral economics as a function of expectations and outcomes combined, rather than simple pleasure, just like we think of dopamine.

Chapter 3: Economic Implications of Reference Dependence

Another key theory of behavioral economics, for which Daniel Kahneman won the 2002 Nobel Prize in Economics, is prospect theory. You might remember that economic models tend to be designed to describe what people *should* do; prospect theory describes what they actually *will* do. Basically, prospect theory is that people decide which choice to make based on the potential net value (the sum of positive and negative value), rather than on the actual outcomes, and that they use some sort of logical system, or heuristic, to determine this. Economics tends to presuppose that people already know which choice is better for them, that they'll choose to place their money in a savings account instead of play small odds at a casino to double it. But prospect theory allows for what many people do in real life, which is choose the gamble *because* of the net value. Prospect theory adapts to the way our brains actually work.[xii]

Prospect theory relies on reference dependence and probability weighting. We will talk about probability weighting in the next chapter, so for now, let's focus in more on reference dependence. In the previous chapter, we went over a broad definition and then the neurochemical underpinnings of reference dependence. Here, we will discuss its economic and behavioral implications in more detail.

Reference dependence causes a lot of our major biases, but it can also help us make good decisions. It is always important to remember that our brains are wired the way they are for a reason, and that this reason is generally to help us survive and continue the species. We have already talked about how dopamine neurons react to disappointments or met expectations. One new scenario is that when a reward is totally predictable, in that the person already knows it is coming, the firing rate of the neurons stays constant. This relationship of the reward to the expectations of the reward is called the reward prediction error. "Error" here does not mean that something wrong occurred, but instead merely means the amount the reward deviated from expectations of the reward.

Prediction error occurs precisely because of how dopamine works in the brain. When Pavlov conditioned his dogs to expect a treat after a bell, their dopamine neurons initially reacted to the treat. However, when the bell predicts the treat enough times, the dopamine neurons actually began to respond to the sound of the bell, which is less predictable than the treat that always comes after the bell. Dopamine reacts more to happy surprises than happy results. Furthermore, if the bell rings but then a treat does not come, the dopamine neurons react in a negative manner because they are "disappointed." They also lack any sort of reaction when the expected reward is received. We can call the "happy surprise" a positive error, the "disappointment" a negative error, and the neutral outcome no error. All of these fall under the term "prediction error." Prediction error is part of what creates addictive behavior in humans; chasing positive error, those rushes of dopamine, can lead to serious substance abuse problems that become worse and worse as the body becomes habituated to new "rewards" in the form of substances.

The endowment effect, meanwhile, explains our emotional reactions to things we become "attached" to. Even if something is not very valuable, such as a child's handmade ornament, we value it more than we rationally should and will take actions in order not to lose it. It is caused by two psychological principles called loss aversion and ownership.[xiii] Loss aversion occurs for much the same reason we experience deep disappointment during a negative error in prediction: the pain we feel when we lose something is twice as deep as the pleasure we feel at gaining the thing.[xiv] Ownership, meanwhile, is exactly what it sounds like: once we feel that we have something, we love it even more and will take extraordinary action to retain it, to the point of refusing to trade it for something equally as valuable or paying more to keep the item than we would to buy a new one. This is why on the television program *Love It or List It,* for example, people mostly decide to keep their renovated house instead of buying one of the new ones on offer, even if a new house would be in a better location and offers more of the amenities they want. In a more extreme example, hoarders experience extreme "ownership" because they become so attached to their stuff they cannot bear to part with it—even the stuff that most people would categorize as garbage.

Reference dependence is at the root of this kind of bias. People become attached to what they know and are familiar with because it helps orient them in their world. This attachment is also called the "endowment effect." The endowment effect has had a large impact on the field of behavioral economics and economics as a whole because it helped explain strange behaviors in the market, like refusal to trade even though the two items have the same value. One of these specific odd behaviors was described in a recent paper by Santosh Anagol and his team, who found that IPOs in India are influenced by the endowment effect. In India, shares of IPOs are given out in a lottery system when too many people subscribe to them. People who win the lottery get a certain number of shares, while people who aren't selected don't get any shares and have to buy them after the company starts trading. Logically, then, all investors would equally want to have shares when they participate in the IPO. However, according to the study, this did not happen. Instead, only 1% of the lottery's losers had purchased shares in the year following the IPO, while 62.4% of the winners had held on to their shares. Two years after the IPO, only 1.7% of the lottery losers had bought shares, while 36% of the winners kept theirs. There was no relationship between these results and the price movements, so the investors had no rational reason to behave this way. Instead, the endowment effect biased them toward the status quo at the IPO; they did not buy the shares they had wanted even after they were able to.[xv]

The endowment effect also keeps people attached to things. Let's say you were shopping for a new phone, so the salesperson guided you to the latest iPhone. After playing with it, you decide that you want it, even though you didn't want to spend so much on a new phone. The salesperson was taking advantage of the endowment effect. You would have been unlikely to buy the brand new phone if you had looked over an online catalogue, for example, because you wouldn't have been attached to the new product and would have been thinking more rationally about your money. However, because you got the experience of "ownership" of the newer phone, you experienced the endowment effect and wanted it to be yours more. Furthermore, you'd be more upset if you sold your phone or if it was stolen because of this sense of ownership. This is how powerful the endowment effect is.

The amount of money you'd take to part with your new iPhone is called the "willingness to accept," which is measured by the level of some benefit (in this case, money) you would take to do something. There is also a corresponding value called "willingness to pay," which is how much value someone is willing to sacrifice for some good, service, or benefit. Willingness to pay is limited by personal wealth, but willingness to accept has no theoretical limit. When there is a discrepancy between these two metrics—for example, you are willing to accept far more money than someone is willing to pay for what you are exchanging—markets behave inefficiently. If people don't want to pay more than $500 for your phone, but you don't want to sell it for less than $800, your phone won't change hands and the market for it will be inefficient.

This happens on a larger scale, too. If there were 200 free tickets available to students for a college football game, but they were selected randomly from the student body, economists would say that students who wanted to go to the game but weren't selected would buy tickets from students willing to sell them. However, things don't always happen this way. Real life marketplaces are much more inefficient. Take, for example, a 1996 study by Dan Ariely and Ziv Carmon on Duke basketball tickets. The researchers called 100 students who were in the ticket lottery for the Final Four NCAA basketball tournament game, some of whom lost and some of whom won. When the researchers asked the students who lost how much they'd pay for a ticket, the average amount was $150. However, the average sale price for tickets was $2,400, which is much higher than what the surveyed students were willing to pay! The randomness of the lottery changed how much people were willing to pay. While the students who won tickets thought of it as a unique experience that they would remember for the rest of their lives, the students who lost viewed it as just another sports ticket; they consoled themselves with the idea that they weren't missing out on much. When Ariely and Carmon tested their hypothesis again, they asked students to judge the value of the tickets based on experience instead of money. Paradoxically, this made them focus on whether they would lose money by selling or buying tickets, instead of the experience; sellers determined prices based on the prices of other sports tickets.[xvi]

These financial transactions were clearly not thought through in an economically rational way because of the endowment effect once students had tickets in their possession. The disparity in valuation between the two groups caused inefficiencies in the market and the distribution of tickets according to value. This is true in other scenarios, too. You might remember the incident on a United Airlines plane where a man was forcibly dragged away from his seat because airline employees wanted to take the flight. Even though airlines generally offer passengers financial compensation or a different ticket at no cost when they bump them from flights, when they sit down, the endowment effect makes them more attached to their seats and that specific flight by setting expectations for travel. This causes inefficiencies in how different parties view the value of the seats, which is how people end up being dragged off a plane down the middle of an aisle.

This can be hard to understand, because it seems like so much difficulty for such a relatively insignificant good. However, imagine that you found a twenty-dollar bill on the ground on your way to work. You then pass a sale that is offering dresses discounted at $20. Although you might have stopped in the store before, you'd be unlikely to use the $20 you found on the sale. Instead, you'd want to save it for something really special, right? Even though it's just a twenty-dollar bill?

Believe it or not, you have just fallen prey to the endowment effect.

Several scientists have proposed theoretical explanations for the endowment effect. Kahneman has proposed that the effect is caused by loss aversion, which causes resistance to any sort of loss and can affect willingness to accept. This hypothesis, however, is not universally accepted by social scientists. David Gal has proposed a theory of psychological inertia as an explanation, wherein imprecise valuation by both sellers and buyers lead to inefficiencies and price discrepancies because the value is not sufficient for both parties to be willing to make an exchange. Psychologists have also argued that the roots of the endowment effect are connected through self-identification with the object. Cognitive scientists have theorized that our information processing is biased toward acquisition because it makes information easier to obtain, or that the endowment effect is a function of reference dependence, and evolutionary biologists have proposed that it is an evolved trait that helped survival in barter scenarios.[xvii]

However, the theory that we will explore in more detail is loss aversion. Reference dependence favors loss aversion; our losses affect us more than our gains, and they also have a bigger impact as past experiences. Kahneman and Tversky conducted a study that demonstrates this phenomenon; they found that people tend to find loss twice as painful as they find gain pleasurable. Thus, people will take more risks to avoid loss than they will to gain value, even though the loss and the gain might be economically the same. To assess this, Kahneman and Tversky created a coin flip scenario. They constructed a game where people started with an initial sum, say, $50,000. They then presented them with two options: either to give them more money, say, another $50,000, or they let them flip a coin. If the coin landed on heads, the subject would win even *more* money, $100,000 for example. But if it landed on tails, the subject would get no extra money. Thus the options were getting $100,000, $150,000, or $50,000 if they lost the toss. People would generally choose not to flip the coin. However, if the subjects were initially given $100,000, and the two options were either a guaranteed loss of $25,000 or the coin toss scenario, people would generally choose to flip the coin. Mathematically, the odds of loss or gain are the same in both scenarios. However, the desire to avoid losing money drives the decision to take more risk in the second scenario. People want to avoid loss if it's certain, even if they will possibly end up with less money. Of course, this doesn't apply to everyone. But it applies to most people.[xviii]

Over time, researchers were able to calculate the gain-loss ratio that people found acceptable to begin to play the game. This ratio is slightly less than 2:1, which means that loss has about twice as much of an influence on decision-making as gain does for most people. This has been intuitively explored by politicians and advertising. They know that people want to avoid losing what they have and know, like their private health insurance, or their safe neighborhoods. This, of course, all comes back to reference dependence. Because people create their worlds based on private experience, they will generally want to keep their worlds as familiar as possible. Reference dependence is so deeply baked into human nature that we can only work around this.

One of the ways to work around reference dependence is to shift our points of reference, or, as many people would put it, changing our point of view. People might initially be inclined to vote against a candidate advocating for universal government-provided healthcare. They want to protect the medical care they have, because they would feel unsafe without it. Furthermore, many people understand their private plans, but don't know what benefits public health insurance would entail. This fear of the unknown, and reliance on reference dependence, can be a powerful force.

However, shifting one's reference dependence could change one's opinion on the issue. Someone might examine a candidate's plan to implement universal healthcare and what effect it would have on the medical system. They could also educate themselves about how many people are struggling with medical bills due to private insurance, and the extreme cost of treatments for chronic conditions and diseases. They could even travel to countries with public healthcare to see an example of how the system works. All this could make them more accepting of the newness of a public health plan, and more willing to vote for it.

You can also avoid being tricked by reference dependence by putting things into perspective, by weighing small consequences against large ones. While giving up private insurance might be scary because your care system could change, the positive changes it would bring to people who can't afford medical care but don't qualify for public assistance outweigh this because of their larger benefit to overall society and productivity.

Finally, consider the alternatives and other possible scenarios. Imagine you were diagnosed with cancer, and had to undergo treatment while also quitting your job. Your medical bills are massive, but you have no way to pay them. Think about the opportunity cost of public health insurance in this scenario; while you'd give up the private benefits you enjoy in everyday life, you'd be in a better financial position if you became seriously ill. This alternate reference point helps you see the issue from other angles. Economics is a social science, which means it is concerned with all of society. Seeing other viewpoints in society, or imagining yourself in a different life situation, can actually help you improve your decisions from an economic standpoint. You will be better able to evaluate overall utility and tailor your decisions to generate more value for yourself and society at large.

Chapter 4: Probability Weighting

Probability weighting is the other key concept behind prospect theory, so it is important that we explore it as much as we explored reference dependence in our understanding of behavioral economics. Probability weighting describes the biases people hold when deciding the probability of things that are going to happen. These are behind why we often make mistakes when guessing probability of events.

Probability is defined as the likelihood that something—which must be a definite thing—will occur. We describe it using either percentages or frequency, which will always correspond fractionally: if you make a basket in basketball 80% of the time, you make it an average of 4 out of 5 times. These descriptions are both quantitative; they turn likelihood into numerical chances. Probability, because it is a fraction, will always be between 0 and 1, which represent impossible and certain cases respectively. Probability theory describes probability with mathematical formulas, and is used in every quantitatively-oriented field including economics and statistics. Probability helps us describe the frequency of future events and even the outcomes of complex systems, which tend to behave in fairly unpredictable ways.[xix]

Probability can be easy to describe, as in the case of a coin toss; there is a 50% chance that either side will come out on top after the flip. This is an exclusive probability, because either one or the other can happen, but not both. However, real-world probabilities are not always so neat. Things like subway times or weather are hard to predict because the probabilities can change so quickly.

There are many different moving parts, and any of them could have an effect on the probability of a certain event.

Behavioral economists call these complicated moving parts "probability weights." This refers to how much influence each factor has on a probability. Think of a heavy backpack. A large book will probably contribute more to the weight than a pack of tissues. The different factors in probability weights work the same way. Probabilities can be overweighted and underweighted; this means that they are misjudged as either too important to the outcome, or not important enough.

Rational people would give probabilities weights based on a system that is consistent and complete. Objective numerical values—for example, something being twice as likely as something else in the sense of 40% vs. 20%—

should correspond to the subjective probability, so that the weighting in a decision corresponds to the weighting in the numbers. Completeness in probability weighting just means that all the different probabilities should always add up to 100%.

However, people tend to be poor judges of subjective vs. objective probability. Although they should theoretically make a choice that has proportionality with the subjective probability of, say, utility, in reality their probabilities tend to be inconsistent, incomplete, or disproportionate. This happens because people rely on their personal experiences. They fall victim to reference dependence. A better heuristic would be to imagine a scenario for the probabilities of what might happen with a given choice, and the more vivid and realistic, the more likely this probability is to happen. This is called the availability heuristic, and is essentially the idea that the mind will fixate on or remember something because it is important.

Availability heuristic is a huge bias for our brains; we tend to intuit our most important memories based on the ones that stick around, even though this might not always be the case. Your most "important" point of reference for a decision might not necessarily be the most helpful one. This bias even shows up in "objective," experimental scientific studies, and affects every aspect of people's lives. People tend to judge crime, for example, by the number of murders in a city, even though there are many other indicators of crime. This is because murders are the most vivid crimes our brains can process, and so they tend to "stick" and become our brain's default yardstick even though they are a highly specialized and relatively rare crime. Thus crime statistics often tend to be murder statistics, despite the fact that this is not representative of all crime.[xx]

Objective probabilities all have corresponding subjective probability weights. It can be hard to fit quantitative probabilities into decision-making, and we often have a mismatch between the two types. It is therefore important to first outline the different objective probabilities and their corresponding subjective probabilities,

Events with a low probability fall below a 25% chance of occurring. This means that they are unlikely to happen, but they still have a large effect on people's decision-making. Even though plane crashes have a low probability of happening, the fear of a crash keeps many people from flying as a method of travel, because they weight the subjective probability of a crash higher than the objective probability. Even though a plane crash might have a 0.01% chance of happening, people with a fear of flying will put that chance at, for example, 30% subjectively. People tend to do this for other scenarios as well. Even though you're extremely unlikely to win big in a casino, people still gamble huge sums of money on high-stakes games because they see the subjective probability of winning as higher than what the objective probability actually is.

In 1654, the mathematician Blaise Pascal described a formula to describe the probability of winning the lottery in terms of time and expected value. The probability of winning the lottery is about the same as randomly picking a second from all the time between now and 1654 and getting the moment you were born, but people still play the lottery because the expected value is higher and diminishes slowly over time. However, these are not the only factors contributing to the popularity of the lottery and gambling. Dopamine, as we have learned, responds well to anticipation and expectations of reward, getting us hooked on the feeling of winning. People's fantasies about what they will do with winnings are also a large motivating factor, as is the social community provided by being around other gamblers or lottery players. Since the lottery costs little to play and provides big winnings, it's not necessarily irrational to play, but it is an example of overweighting in subjective probability.

Events with an intermediate probability have a 25 to 75% chance of occurring. They might happen or they might not, it's difficult to tell. For this reason, the probability weighting function goes flat here. Objective probability changes don't affect subjective probability much in this range. Let's say, for example, that there is a 60% chance of rain for the day, and you forgot your umbrella. You can buy one on the way to work, or you can go straight there, not spend the money, and take your chances. While you're walking to work, the chance is altered to 70%. You're unlikely to change your mind based on the new weather report, because in this probability range, such a small change won't affect how your brain thinks of the subjective probability. There is still a 30% chance it won't rain; why spend money to avoid getting rained on when you still have such a high probability that you won't even have to deal with it?

This does not mean that these percentage changes don't matter; they do. It simply means that they tend to have less influence on our decisions when they occur in this range. Between 25 and 75% probability, every 2% difference in objective probability corresponds to a little less than 1% change in subjective probability. In other words, changes in objective probability in the middle range don't proportionally affect how we see that probability; in fact, it has such a small effect that our brains will underestimate the change in probability by half of what the change actually was.

High-probability events, or those with a probability greater than 75%, are more likely than not to happen, although they still could not (with the exception of events that are certain to happen with 100% probability, of course). High objective probabilities have the inverse effect on subjective probabilities as low-range objective probabilities do: they lead people to perceive them as less likely to happen than they actually are. If there is a 90% chance of rain, for example, your brain perceives it as about 75%, and even 99% chances are underestimated as around 95%.

This manifests itself in the real world as people taking fewer risks when things are more likely to go their way. For example, even though you are relatively unlikely to contract colon cancer in your lifetime, doctors still recommend and perform regular colonoscopies when people reach their 50s. Even though Peter Thiel is more physically fit and probably has a longer life expectancy than most people, he is still famously seeking supposedly life-extending treatments like injecting himself with the blood of younger people. This is all connected to loss aversion; the more likely something becomes, the more people want to avoid losing it, so they will take extra measures to make sure it doesn't happen.

People's subjective reactions to low, mid-range, and high objective probabilities form the probability weighting aspect of prospect theory. This causes us to make irrational decisions because we cannot accurately judge probability; we think low-probability events like plane crashes are more likely to happen to us than they actually are, we don't really pay attention to events with a medium probability, and we act as if high-probability events are less likely to happen than they are. In other words, we are terrible judges of the probability of things happening to us.

So, how do we deal with these error-causing biases? The narratives our brains create about the probability of various future events happening to us can be very powerful. However, there are some strategies for working around these perceptive tendencies. The first strategy you can use is working *with* availability heuristics, instead of against them. Instead of vividly imagining a plane crash—a low-probability event—and convincing yourself it will happen to you, imagine it in a less realistic, more cartoonish way. Mental distancing can also help; imagine you're reading a news report about it happening to someone else, instead of actually being in the crashing plane, or imagine that it's taking place in a movie. Imagining these scenarios will, paradoxically, give you a more realistic picture of the likelihood of a plane crash happening to you.

Medium-probability events can be an especially difficult problem because our brains tend to ignore them. You can think about these events as the frequency of something happening, instead of how likely it is to happen to *you* specifically. For every 5 people who eat the recalled lettuce you saw on the news, 1 of them will statistically contract salmonella. Thinking of four other people you know isn't very hard, and if you eat the lettuce, you could easily be the one who gets food poisoning! Thinking of this probability in tangible, real-world terms instead of abstract statistics drives the reality home that this lettuce is very dangerous and has made a lot of people sick, and that you could easily be one of those people if you eat it. It's therefore for the best that you just throw it out instead of chancing it. Remember, objective evidence is your friend when it comes to subjective probabilities. Our brains don't always do well with abstract concepts and numbers; applying numbers to real-world evidence can help correct your perceptions of real-world objective probabilities.

Chapter 5: Risk

So far, we've talked about several of the underlying components of human behavior and the theory of behavioral economics. However, we have not talked about a common subject that forms the foundation of everything we've discussed thus far: risk. Some people love risk, and some people hate it, but we all have to live with it. This chapter will focus on what risk is, how it works in our lives, and how we can manage it and harness it to benefit us.

While the common usage of "risk" seems to imply a meaning of "dangerous," in economics it simply means the presence of multiple outcomes from a choice that have different values. Another important component of economic risk is whether or not we know the probabilities behind different outcomes, or whether we can estimate these probabilities. If we can know or estimate probabilities, then the choice has risk involved. If we can't, the outcomes have *ambiguity*, not risk. Risk doesn't have to involve rappelling down the side of a mountain or diving to the bottom of the ocean in a submarine; in fact, it underlies most of what we do, even if our choices can only lead to good or neutral outcomes.

People tend to behave in three different ways when making economic decisions: risk-seeking, risk-neutral, or risk-averse. As you might expect, most people favor risk-averse choices, where they choose the more secure, safer option over the riskier one, especially when each outcome has the same expected value. Risk aversion is defined as people's efforts to lower uncertainty in economic decisions. People always try to choose the more "known" option, or to find more information about the things that are uncertain. Risk-averse investors, for example, tend to choose accounts that have more stable stock investments and generate less interest, but are also less likely to lose money as the reliability of the stocks chosen is better known. You might choose an account that generates 5% interest from more stable investments over one that has the *possibility* of generating 20% interest, or crashing, because the investments in the portfolio are overall less stable. Even though you could make more money, you could also lose a lot of money with the second portfolio, and as we've already mentioned, people tend to be guided by loss aversion in their decisions.[xxi]

A risk-seeking person, of course, would pick the option with the possibility of generating higher interest payments. Meanwhile, a risk-neutral person would be indifferent between the two options, and be fine with either one. The amount of the payoff can also change people's amenability to risk. For example, if the average payoff of the higher-risk investment was $1,000, and the minimum amount of money that someone would accept instead of making the bet was $900, this amount—$900—is called the certainty equivalent. The difference between these two numbers, which is $100 in this case, is the risk premium. Since the risk premium is positive here, the person is risk-averse. Risk-neutral people have a risk premium of 0, and risk-seeking people have a premium that is negative.

While value of different risks is easy to determine in an investment context, it is more difficult to determine when it comes to more subjective qualities. We can use an equation called a utility function to find how much subjective value someone would derive from a quantitative result like monetary value. Economists have figured out that people give money a subjective value, along with how much it is quantitatively worth. Furthermore, they figured out that people's subjective value had diminishing marginal utility, or that people derive less and less satisfaction from money the more they have of it. Originally this was described in terms of wealth; we can all agree that a dollar is worth more to a person in poverty than a wealthy person with plenty of money. Prospect theory doesn't follow this more traditional definition, but it does maintain the foundation of diminishing marginal utility. For example, eating one Big Mac when you're hungry is highly satisfying, but eating five in a row makes you feel more and more sick the more you eat. This fundamental aspect of human nature feeds directly into our propensity for risk-averse behavior.

If I offered you the option of either shooting a half-court basket to win $3000, but if you miss you get nothing, or a guaranteed payment of $1500, you'd most likely take the $1500. Think about why you made this choice. Even though the $1500 seems more likely, really, the average winnings from the half-court shot would be larger. However, the $1500 is more appealing because of diminishing marginal utility. Subjectively, the option of either having zero or $3000 is a much bigger difference than the difference between not playing and having $1500 or winning and having $3000. If you have diminishing marginal utility for money, which most people do, you will be risk-averse. This is why most people tend to exhibit risk-averse behavior.

Furthermore, people often tend to be risk-averse even when dealing with smaller amounts of money. They will avoid risk even when only $20 is at stake, and risk aversion only increases with the amount of money involved. This was proven by economist Matthew Rabin, who in his research found that risk aversion only increases with stakes if people exhibit it with smaller amounts of money. Therefore, something other than diminishing marginal utility must be in play.[xxii]

This is where we really come back to loss aversion. When people think of risk in terms of losing and gaining, they tend to exhibit more characteristics of loss aversion. This is because they hold the less risky choice as their reference point, which changes their perspective. Their subjective assessment of loss affects their perception of the actual risk, and it will be more powerful than the possibility of gaining from the risk taken.

Risk aversion is not necessarily a bad thing in economic models. In fact, risk-seeking behavior often leads to market inefficiencies. Think of a gambling addict. This person will go back to the casino again and again no matter how much money they lose, and end up being exploited by gambling businesses. A risk-seeking person is the same way; people will notice their behavior and use it to take more and more money away from them in things like financial schemes and other types of scams.

However, situations involving losses are a bit trickier. Think of a scenario where the choices were either a sure loss, or the possibility of either losing *more* or losing *nothing*. You might think that people would be even more risk-averse when it comes to losses. However, behavioral economics has found a different answer. According to prospect theory, we all have diminishing marginal utility for monetary gains *and* losses. Imagine another game where you have the option of either losing $1500 or flipping a coin to decide whether you lose $1600 or nothing. While the difference between losing $0 and $1600 seems like a lot, the difference between losing

$1500 and $1600 doesn't. Therefore, you'd probably actually choose the *riskier* option, because it offers the possibility of losing nothing. This follows people's general behavior patterns around risk; they are averse to risk when there is gain involved, but seek out risk when there is loss involved.

People's attitude toward risk is also inconsistent. Just because someone is risk-averse in their financial decisions does not mean they avoid risk in things like travel or activities. Paragliding could be their favorite activity! This is because people's level of risk behavior in different aspects of their lives are not correlated with each other. People can be universally risk-averse, but they can also view the benefits of different risks and different activities differently. In a study, psychologist Elke Weber found exactly this result: people's different perceptions and practices of activities varied based on a combination of how they viewed the benefits and risks. This explains why someone would go cliff diving but not invest in a startup's IPO. They simply view the risk/benefit balance for each of these things differently.

The main takeaways from Weber's work are that risk preferences are not unilateral in people, and that our attitudes and practices with regards to risk rely on our perception of the rewards and probabilities inherent in a risk. This underscores just how influential our reference points are, and how much our subjective probability assessments can vary from person to person. Our evaluations of risk are highly individualized and based on our personal set of biases.

Of course, risk is not inherently bad. It can sometimes lead to big payoffs, and people who have more aggressive and risky stock portfolios tend to make more money overall than those with more conservative portfolios. The first thing you can do to minimize your risk and make sure you don't lose your shirt, literally or metaphorically, is to do exactly what investment advisors do: diversify your levels of risk.

The theory of portfolio diversification was developed by the economist Harry Markowitz in 1951, who came up with the idea that assets in a portfolio shouldn't all be the same kind that change at the same time. Instead, they should change at different times to minimize the impact of stock market swings. This way, even if one investment collapses, you still have all the other ones in your portfolio. The combined risk of your investments is the portfolio's overall risk, and you can work to make this total risk as low as possible while still keeping some risky investments. This is called modern portfolio theory, and it's an underlying principle of investment strategy today.[xxiii]

Modern portfolio theory relies on clinical psychology in addition to economics, in that it's designed to keep people from having overly emotional reactions to the whims of the market. Modern portfolio theory is designed to reduce people's regret at making risky investments that don't pan out, so their emotions don't bias their future investment choices. Psychologists and economists also advise "thinking like a trader" to help with sensible portfolio management, which essentially means looking at a portfolio from a distance, with a more analytical than emotional eye. This means looking at losses as a small component of the whole, and looking at the portfolio's long-term performance instead of its day-to-day value. Taking these viewpoints will help you make decisions that benefit the long-term growth of the investment, and prevent irrational decisions based on loss avoidance, subjective probability, and the endowment effect.

Chapter 6: Comparison

Recent research has found that our brains construct value itself in a highly subjective way. This value construction happens every day, for even the most minor of decisions. Value isn't a stable quantity. Your own value for a given object or experience can change based on your circumstances and reference points.

Part of how we construct value is through a theory called constructed preferences. The idea behind this is that our brains assign things subjective value when they need it. Although economists have not accepted this theory, psychologists do believe it has validity—and since behavioral economics has such a large psychological component, it's important to thinking about how our brains make decisions. We construct subjective value by going through something called the "decision problem" in our heads, which is essentially the process of going through all the separate parts of our memories to make a decision. Naturally, this leads to a large bias in the constructed value.

There are also specific biases called "decision biases" at work during this process. The first decision bias is the decoy effect.[xxiv] The decoy effect happens when we are trying to choose between two options and a third is introduced that we did not choose. This third option can create a bias toward the choice that seems better in comparison to the third "decoy" option. The decoy effect is commonly used in marketing. If you are trying to choose between a laptop with 50 GB of storage and a more expensive one with 100 GB of storage, the introduction of a 75 GB laptop with a more expensive price tag than either other option can guide people toward the 100 GB laptop, which is better than the decoy option in both storage space and price.

Airlines also use decoys in this way. By offering Basic Economy, Economy, and Premium Economy fares, airlines have been able to charge more for tickets in coach class by steering people toward Premium, which has small benefits like a checked bag and extra legroom compared to normal economy, and away from Economy, which often lacks those amenities, with a Basic option that is obviously worse than both. The Basic option makes people think about the benefits they'll get if they spend just a little more on Premium, and totally biases them against the no-frills Basic and the mid-range Economy. Giving a Basic option leads to more people buying more expensive Economy tickets.

The decoy effect can also be present in elections; many people blamed Bernie Sanders's candidacy for Hillary Clinton's loss in the 2016 presidential election, because it pushed people away from the Democratic Party and towards Trump because of their dislike for Clinton. Similar effects were seen in elections with a third party candidate, famously in the cases of Ralph Nader and Ross Perot. These third options can be highly disruptive to people's decision-making.

The second type of decision bias is the compromise effect.[xxv] This is exactly what it sounds like: when no option sticks out as clearly and objectively better or worse, our natures tend toward compromise and will pick a third, middle option. For example, many restaurants will also put expensive food at the top of the menu and cheap food at the bottom, so that people will pick a middle option that is still expensive. You might not want the oysters, but you also don't necessarily want a chicken recipe you can get at home, so you go with a pricier steak. Restaurants also do this with their wine list, so that people will spend more on a bottle of wine than they normally would in an effort to seem reasonable in their spending while still making the evening special. It is important to remember that compromise is not necessarily our friend; sometimes it just means we don't get what we want, and no one is happy with the conclusion reached as they still felt they spent too much money, or not enough. The best solution is to be more strategic—treat yourself sometimes, and stay financially prudent other times. This way, you'll be happier with your choices, and avoid paying more for things than you want to just to seem reasonable.

If we are subject to so much bias and inconsistency, why do our brains even try to construct value? The answer lies in a few different places. First of all, we have biases for a reason:

they do actually aid in decision-making. It can be overwhelming to decide between two options that both have pros and cons. Your biases can help sort through all this information and figure out what you're likely to prioritize, and what is likely to cause you regret. We can't agonize over every decision in our lives; think of how unhappy the character Chidi is in *The Good Place*! Biases help us actually get on with our lives instead of spending all our time going through decision processes.

Our brains also construct preferences because they have to. *Tons* of information go into every decision we make, and we can't possibly pay attention to all of it. Constructing value gives us a system by which we can evaluate the relevance and importance of all this information to make a more "educated" decision.

Antonio Rangel and Hilke Plassman work precisely at the intersection between economics and neuroscience, where behavioral economics falls. They have conducted several experiments on how the brain calculates and conceives value. One of these experiments involved hunger. Study participants arrived hungry, were put in an MRI machine, and then shown photos of brand-name snacks. They then had to record how much they would pay for the snack. After the MRI, still having not eaten, the participants would be offered a snack by the research team, who would sell it to them for the price the participants said they would pay. The team found that the medial orbitofrontal cortex lit up during the monetary-value assessment of each snack; this part of the brain receives information from the dopamine neurons discussed in previous chapters. Thus, cognitively, dopamine is related to people's willingness to pay, a value which we also discussed earlier that is "encoded" in this region of the brain. This willingness to pay was associated with the reward experienced by the participants.[xxvi]

Furthermore, the region of the brain where willingness to pay was encoded lit up more the more monetary value participants assigned to the snacks. The activity in the brain region also correlated to specific snacks that were the most valuable to the individuals, and there was no overall trend in type. This means that the brain lit up according to the *value* that each participant placed on each snack, which was subjective.

The medial orbitofrontal cortex's activity is therefore known as the "common currency" for subjective value, because it is a metric that works despite people's differing tastes and biases. This "common currency" helps us in the decision-making process. Further studies established that the role of this part of the brain was similar for other goods as well, such as electronics, and not just food. Scientists have concluded that this means that our brains truly use this "common currency" for all goods, even if different pathways are used for different types. It is all processed the same way cognitively.

Later research has focused on whether this process of creating subjective value in the brain is automatic and happens without having to make a conscious choice. Researchers used facial expressions, which tend to be both universal and fairly unconscious, to gauge value assessment in non-choice contexts. In a study, participants were shown faces with a wide variety of attractiveness, and passively received a monetary reward bonus in a fixed amount. The researchers did this to make sure they had a control for how the brain reacts to a variety of faces and how it responds to rewards in the form of money.

The researchers then had participants make *active* choices to spend some of the money the researchers gave them to see attractive faces again. This showed the researchers the monetary value participants assigned to the faces, while also knowing how their brains reacted when they saw the attractive faces, and how much they valued their money (since this is also subjective). The researchers believed that if the brain was building the subjective value of the faces automatically, then the brain activity seen when people look at attractive faces will appear when they view other attractive faces as well. The researchers found that this consistent activity not only occurred, but it also happened in the same region of the brain that lit up when shown the snacks in the other study we mentioned: the medial orbitofrontal cortex. This region therefore seems to be the "common currency" for the brain interpreting value and reward. If someone was willing to pay a lot to see the attractive faces, that region would light up more on the scan because they assigned more value to the faces. If they didn't want to pay much, then that region actually lit up more for the money itself than for the faces. In other words, the researchers showed that this part of the brain determined the subjective value of the money and the faces *in comparison to each other*.

Constructed preferences actually provide our brains with a flexible system to judge the value of different things in our lives. Our preferences change in context; while we might not prefer a salad to a burger for lunch, we could still prefer a salad to porridge as a lunch. The environments and contexts we experience always affect what we value and prefer in our decision-making. These changing levels of value are based on what kind of questions you're asking yourself in your decisions. Fortunately, this means that you actually have a lot of control over what you see as subjective value. This is why people advise making pro-con lists when you're trying to make a big decision; it can change your perspective by prompting different questions about aspects of your decision. Isolating each choice, instead of judging them by comparison, can also contribute to better decision-making. Do you actually want a dress that you see in a store window, or do you just want it because it's on sale? Do you really want ice cream because you are hungry, or is it just because you're strolling the boardwalk at the beach? Asking these kinds of questions can help save you money and, in the case of the ice cream, make you healthier in the long term. It can also help you determine what really matters to you, as opposed to what you think *should* matter.

When choosing between multiple options, removing an option from consideration can also be helpful. Eliminate a third choice when you've narrowed down your top three colleges, and you might be able to make a better choice about what is the right fit for your education and goals. Try to force yourself to choose between two restaurant options instead of having to choose from five, and you might feel more strongly. Conscious elimination of these decoys will help keep your brain from being tricked.

After all, we don't always know what our real priorities are, and it's hard to detect how biases are at work in our day-to-day lives. Being conscious of value construction can help you become more conscious of what matters, and in turn help you build decision-making skills that will better reflect your real priorities. This practice can also help you figure out what to ignore, and what information is irrelevant or unimportant in a decision. We can't be perfect decision makers, but more awareness and control over our cognitive processes can help us be more consistent and efficient in our choices.

Chapter 7: Bounded Rationality

We can make simple decisions based on a simple calculation of benefit vs. risk, and how we value our time. However, complex decisions can also make evaluating these metrics difficult, which is why we need simpler rules to make them. This idea of using a rule to shorten the process of making a complex decision is called bounded rationality, and it is another major principle of behavioral economics. Bounded rationality has the name it does because it is a term for the limits that keep us from being perfectly rational economic actors. These factors include the limits of our cognition, the time we have to consider our options, and how easy the decision is to make. We can only reach the conclusions that come closest to solving the problem, not the actual perfect solutions.[xxvii]

The idea of bounded rationality was conceived by Herbert Simon, who proposed it in response to the popularity of mathematical decision-making models in academic disciplines. It does not contradict the theory that rationality is the brain's way of optimizing benefits and outcomes. Instead, it simply augments this theory to make it more applicable to the real world. Simon wrote that decision-making is like using a pair of scissors where one blade is human "cognitive limitations" and the other is the structure of our context and surroundings. Essentially, these "scissors" are a tool that takes cognitive limitations into account and compensates for them with known quantities. The components of bounded rationality, if we think of it as a tool or a workaround, are called limited search and satisficing. These ideas were put forth in Simon's 1955 paper, "A Behavioral Model of Rational Choice."[xxviii]

Limited search is the "cognitive limitations" blade of Simon's scissors. Our brains take a *lot* of energy to perform everyday tasks; this is why we need sleep and food to survive! This massive amount of energy required for even ordinary processing means that our brains want to be as efficient in using energy to make decisions as possible. While computational limitations might sound like a bad thing, they actually help us. Think of your brain like a laptop. When you try to do too many things on your laptop, like play videos and scroll through websites with lots of ads at the same time, your laptop gets hot and the fan starts going to cool off the circuits. Your brain is the same way; it *can't* process everything you want it to, because that would require way too much power. So, they simplify things. This simplification takes the form of biases, selective perception, and even the act of focusing.

This simplification is good for our brains, but it is also subject to lots of errors. If you filter out the wrong information—for example, looking at your phone while crossing the street instead of looking for oncoming cars—you can make a lot of mistakes, and in this case even get hit by a car! Thus it is clear that our brains' main challenge is choosing the *right* information to filter. If you think about it, our brains mostly meet this challenge, and this is because of the second scissor blade: the structure of our environment.

Structure is exactly what it sounds like; it is composed of the stable parts of our world. Just like work or school generally structures our days, various factors structure our world and immediate environment, which helps us simplify complex circumstances, just like the structure of a workday helps simplify the tasks you need to do. The first important aspect of structure is that the world is a stable place. There is a reason you generally don't think about or notice when you blink—in the moment your eyes are closed, the world around you doesn't change much. Any changes are so minor that your brain glosses over them and you have a continuous perception of the world around you.

The second aspect of environmental structure is that the changes that do happen in the world are generally predictable. Our brains can predict what will happen next based on new information pretty reliably. For example, if you see thunderclouds in the distance, you know that a storm is coming soon, because your brain knows what that looks like and what it leads to from prior experience. The basic physical laws of our universe don't change, and our brains acquaint themselves with human behavior from the moment we're born, so it is actually fairly easy to predict most everyday occurrences.

Structure helps us make decisions every day. Our brains learn to make decisions within the structure of the scientific laws of the universe, and our processes reflect that. However, making decisions about mortgage refinancing or investing are much more difficult, because they involve abstract informational structures and laws that are harder for our brains to understand. What helps us make decisions as we go about our everyday lives might not be as helpful in more abstract, complex contexts.

Say, for example, that you want to buy a house. Assuming you know where you want to live and what your budget is, you'd still have a lot of options! Each house has its own set of pros and cons, and it's important to pay attention to many different factors such as commute time, noise, the amount of land you get, the neighborhood, value projections, renovations, in-home washers and dryers, air conditioning... the list goes on and on! You can't look at every single house up for sale in the area where you want to live and make a good decision. It's simply not in our brains' power to do so; we have other concerns too!

How would you end up with the best house for you, then? The first step in looking for a home, of course, is house hunting. Behavioral economists call this the search process; although in this case the definition ends up being quite literal, in most case this just means exploring the options available to you. You have to explore these options by learning about many different houses and narrowing your search. This is why realtors advise people to be very specific about what they want in a property. If you want four bedrooms, you're not going to waste your time looking at two-bedroom places, even if they have all the other qualities you want. Narrowing down options according to desired qualities will eliminate a lot of the background noise of the decision-making process.

After you narrow down the houses to three or four that you like, you should find another way to choose among them. If you were an economist's dream decision-maker, you would make a list of every single pro and con and decide what gives you the most utility based on how they interact. However, this process, while the most "rational," is not feasible in real life. Simon realized in his work that making a perfectly "rational" decision would take a lot of time and mental energy, and also actually work against people by making them focus too much on minor aspects of the choices. This is why people get so bogged down by the paint colors they see in homes on the show *House Hunters*. They're encouraged to evaluate every single aspect of the house, because that makes for good television, but it also makes for a murkier decision-making process.

Instead of the *House Hunters* approach, Simon devised a method that he called "satisficing," a portmanteau of "satisfying" and "suffice." Satisficing is essentially the idea that something fits enough of your standards to be *good enough* to be the final choice. If you've narrowed down your search to three houses, there are probably a few features that are really important to you, such as the newness of the house, or the location, or the size of the kitchen. Simon wrote that for each of these important features, people practicing satisficing decision-making should have an "aspirational" level of the feature in mind. They should then evaluate each option based on its relation to the "aspirational" case. A house that was renovated ten years ago might be "new enough" for you, and the commute might be "easy enough" to your job.

Once people use this metric, there is generally one option that stands out as having the attributes that are closest to the ideal. You have found a house that is good enough to suit your needs and wants. This method is relatively simple and easy and often works, but it isn't the best way to make a decision. Your brain can still make mistakes because it can't see the forest for the trees. You might not choose a house you really love out of a desire to "compromise" to get the *overall* closest to your aspirations. Meanwhile, that house that was far away from work was perfect for you in every other way; it's been renovated in the last year, and has an enormous kitchen. Let's say the commute is actually not that much longer than the one from the house you chose, that it's about 20 minutes longer. This is a fairly small sacrifice for your dream house, right? But because you were satisficing, your set aspiration level exaggerated this relatively minor difference (which was close to the aspiration) and made you ignore the positive attributes of the other house.

Satisficing isn't meant to be a tool of the perfect economic actor. Its main goal is simplifying our lives to provide us with the most reliable amount of satisfaction possible. It also helps us better work through really complicated decisions, which is why the practice tends to show up in people who are mentally or physically exhausted. It particularly helps in a structured world that works well with our lifestyle, and so it is a function of privilege as well.

Bounded rationality is a crucial idea in an overall understanding of behavioral economics. It takes into account that we are all humans with flaws, not theoretical actors in an economist's equation. Because we are flawed, simplification can help us make complicated decisions that are beyond our ability to decide rationally. However, it is important to remember that this simplification is happening, and that it might actually be leading us astray. Simplification works in familiar contexts, but in new situations it is better to take as much information as possible into account. When there's little at stake in your decision, it is fine to let your brain take the shortcut, and save you time to deal with bigger and better things.

Chapter 8: Social Decisions

Now that we've explored the processes, psychology, and neuroscience behind decision-making, it is important to address one of the most massive influences on our behavior: social settings. When people interact with another person, or with a small group, their decisions change and exhibit interesting changes in behavior. Economists tend to act as if "rational" actors are acting alone. However, as game theory has explored, this is fundamentally untrue. Simplification of decision-making in social settings is actually better, because it allows people to better judge others' actions and get out of their own heads.

Game theory was originally invented as a branch of mathematics, and that is still the category to which it belongs. Economists now use game theory extensively in their research, as it is an excellent example of strategic thinking at play in decisions. "Games" in game theory don't necessarily have to be things like poker. Instead, they are generally some sort of abstract version of a decision-making scenario, wherein there are "players," choices, and consequences.[xxix]

The most famous example of game theory is the prisoner's dilemma. This is a game where two prisoners are incarcerated for committing a crime together. They are each forced to decide whether to pin the crime on their partner or to refuse to talk. If they both inform on their partner, they get a middling sentence. If they both stay quiet, neither of them will have any evidence against them. If one informs on the other, the one who informs is released while the one who stayed quiet will go to prison for life. The challenge is to make the choice that will give you the best outcome, while taking the other player's actions into account.

The dominant strategy here is informing on your partner. When both players pick this option, they both stay in jail, and lose the option to walk free. This scenario is an example of dominant strategy equilibrium, where both players act purely in their own self-interest. Dominant strategy equilibrium tends to be the most "mediocre" result of the game for both players, wherein neither are really happy about how the game ended. However, if people don't work together in a real-life "game," this tends to be the situation that results. Dominant strategy equilibrium is an expected result because of the inherent self-interest baked into human character.[xxx]

There is a similar genre of games for small groups of people, called coordination games. These are games where people get the best result by working together and behaving according to a group strategy, rather than as an individual. These are often used in team-building scenarios. Think, for example, of a game where a ball rests on a pile of strings on the floor. The goal is to get the ball off the floor, but the only way to do that is to lift every string at the same speed and with the same force. The group thus has to coordinate their physical impulses to lift the string so they're the same, even though some people might think the challenge is better accomplished faster and some might think the opposite. If one person doesn't agree to the strategy, the whole game falls apart. Coordination games therefore rely on mutual trust and communication to produce a result the whole group is happy about. This is not just a phenomenon of office team-building, either. We all mutually trust each other that the stock market is operating legally, that businessmen aren't pocketing profits, that banks keep our financial assets secure. When a member or members of our large collective group betray this trust, global recessions and depressions happen. Therefore, coordination games are important in teaching how important our behaviors are in the collective.[xxxi]

Game theory is seductive because it takes complicated human behavior, like war and competition, and makes it into mathematically simple and predictable models. Of course, these models make a lot of assumptions about human behavior. Game theory assumes people are rational, and motivated by self-interest. Furthermore, it assumes that players will play as if other players are also motivated by self-interest. Players cannot communicate verbally or non-verbally and can't strategize together to split any winnings, and there also can't be outside influences in the outcomes. As you can probably tell, this does not necessarily reflect real life.

The assumption that all players are acting rationally is the key here. It allows game theorists to find mathematical solutions for behavioral problems by using game theory, but it also doesn't allow for people who *aren't* acting rationally. Although a game theory player *should* think about how their actions will influence the other players' choices and incorporate this information into their own choices, they don't always have the time or strategic know-how to do this. This is in fact a quite complicated strategy, and it is called backward induction. It is essentially starting with the ideal result in one's mind, and thinking backward through all the steps in the game necessary to reach that result. Economists tend to assume people can perform as much backward induction as is necessary to succeed in the game, but we are limited in assessing how rational people are and what choices they will make. Furthermore, everyone's rationality and thinking processes have different limitations. You can't use how you think as a guide to how other people think, or as a guarantee that they'll act the same way you do. As a result, people tend to pick what they think of as the "safe" option when in a game theory situation.

Similar to this is the theory of the wisdom of crowds. Most people think that crowds are better at making behavioral choices and judging others' behavior. This, after all, is the entire concept behind democracy; the people as a collective are better at choosing their leader than an elite few are, or God. However, this concept clearly has limits.

The wisdom of crowds was first conceived of in 1907 by Francis Galton, who was a British social scientist. He published this idea in the periodical *Nature*, and based his research on what people guessed as the weight of an ox at a livestock show. His sample size was 800 and included everyone from complete amateurs to experts on livestock. The person who guessed the closest would win a substantial prize.

Galton was interested in the fact that while individual guesses varied widely, the median guess value, or the one smack in the middle of the data, was actually very close to what the ox really weighed—it was only nine pounds off. Half of the people guessed more, and half guessed less. Galton proposed that this was because people were aware of other people's guesses, so they guessed in the middle of those because it seemed like the most reasonable option. He called this the *vox populi*, which is Latin for "the voice of the people." This is the exact same concept of the wisdom of crowds. Essentially, the phenomenon of the wisdom of crowds derives from the fact that there is error in everyone's guesses or opinions, but those errors will act as bookends that surround the true value. The middle guess is therefore more likely to be right than any random guess.[xxxii]

It is important to note that Galton used the median guess from the crowd, not the average. The average is limited in that it represents something that doesn't actually exist in the population; it's an amalgamation of every individual component of the same. This is why the average American family has 2.5 children, even though, obviously, no one can have half a child. When people have wildly different opinions or estimates, the median handles the disparate data points better. Another error that might have arisen in this experiment is that people were more likely to trust the opinions of the people in the crowd. However, once a crowd becomes large enough, no experts are necessary. A crowd the size of the one at the livestock show is actually a fairly accurate judge. However, if a crowd gets too big, the size becomes less and less of a helpful factor in judgment as the crowd grows.

Diversity in a crowd also contributes to the wisdom of crowds. Here, diversity means the variety of decision-making styles present in a crowd. Diversity is always relative; we might look for diversity of opinion, diversity of experience, or diversity of intellectual expertise, based on the situation we are in. The natural diversity baked into decision-making will have a large influence on how the group communicates and ultimately what it decides.

Researchers have found that diversity is helpful in group problem-solving situations. Groups and teams that are made up of only high-performing individuals at a given task seem to have lower overall performance than those with more variety in their performance levels. This is because diversity introduces a variety of problem-solving strategies, which allows for more creativity within the group. This effect also increases as the group gets larger. Groups constructed out of a wide variety of personalities also tend to perform better at tasks, because the members are more willing to question and challenge each other, which ultimately leads to better decisions being made.

Even though communication is generally a good thing in group decision-making, social influence can reduce the effects of diversity and the overall wisdom of a crowd. If one particularly influential individual communicates to the group before the decisions are made, diversity in thinking drops, and people adopt the bias introduced by the individual. This is at work in the real world, especially with the advent of political cable news. Networks like Fox have actively biased viewers toward their political stances, and even altered the way they see reality. People also exhibit more confidence in their beliefs and opinions when they receive this kind of non-diverse information, because their influenced views are now also validated. The popular narrative around the world currently despairs at how to undo this kind of bias, but there is a solution, and a surprising one: introducing uninformed people into the group.

The wisdom of the crowd fails in decision-making when the individuals in the crowd are all making the same error. This is due to confidence bias; the more confident people are in their decisions, the less likely they are to notice and fix errors in their decision-making. This kind of overconfidence manifests itself in a "lucky streak" in gambling, or underestimation of an opponent's power in an election. When a crowd is making a good judgment, the more accurate people in the crowd are more confident; when the judgment is wrong, however, the *less* accurate people are more confident. This phenomenon derives from the tendency to believe people who seem more confident, which is a fundamental human behavior. It is also a major driver of systematic bias, and it can completely neuter the wisdom of the crowd.

When people get advice about a decision they are making, they only tend to move toward the suggested decision by a factor of about 25%. This number, meanwhile, is only a composite figure of the three types of advice-takers: those who don't follow advice at all, those who split the difference between their original decision and the advice, and the few who actually follow advice. This is evidence that people are biased *toward* their own judgment; we are all, to some degree, hard-wired for stubbornness. We also tend to value the advice of one confident person over the counsel of a group of people that seem less confident. As a result, we rarely alter our judgments as much as we should because of how our brains process confidence. Even though we might think it does, confidence does not correlate with being correct.

So, how do we harness the wisdom of crowds to our own benefit? It can sometimes steer us toward good decisions, but it can also lead us astray if it's not composed of the right people. The challenge is in being able to judge when the wisdom of the crowd is worth following, and when crowdsourcing will be counterproductive. However, as you might have guessed based on this chapter, there are three good benchmarks to follow. The first is diversity in thought and perspective, which will counteract bias and make people more likely to challenge decisions and reach the best possible one. The next is independent thinking and contribution. Diversity means nothing if people are unwilling to communicate, and an overly confident person can then steer the group towards erroneous judgments. Overcommunication should also be avoided; if people focus too much on getting along or reaching the same conclusion, the positive results of diverse thinking can get lost in attempts toward social cohesion. Groupthink is a powerful thing, and if people do not communicate properly, it can lead to serious decision-making errors.

Even if you don't have a crowd available to you, you can construct one by using a simple decision-making strategy. If you make two guesses about something after considering different viewpoints or taking time to think, the judgment in the middle of those guesses will generally be close to the right one. Getting something on the first guess might be fun, but thinking a little more is more likely to produce the right guess. There is a reason many people with medical problems seek a second opinion; give yourself a second opinion, and you might just come up with the right answer.

Conclusion

The aim of this book is to give you a better, more comprehensible understanding of behavioral economics than more academic papers or textbooks can offer. Behavioral economics is a complex field that integrates neuroscience, mathematics, psychology, and economics, so it might seem esoteric to many. However, it has a lot of relevance in our day-to-day lives, from the most minor of choices (Which tie will I wear today?) to the most serious (Which house will I choose to buy?). Therefore, it is important for everyone to understand how and why their brains think the way they do, and ultimately to use this to their benefit in their decision-making.

In the first chapter, we discussed the definition of behavioral economics and rational choice theory, which is the baseline from which economists study human behavior. While rational choice theory is useful in constructing mathematical economic models, it is a fairly poor model for real human behavior. Behavioral economics was invented to address these gaps, and to explain more of what people decide in real life, as opposed to how they act on paper.

In the second and third chapters, we explored reference dependence in detail. Reference dependence is one of the core ideas behind behavioral economics theory, and posits that people make decisions based on information that they already have. We discussed the influence of dopamine, and how our brains are wired to process dopamine as a function of whether our expectations were met instead of just whether something made us happy. Dopamine not only makes us chase the high of a "happy surprise," which is what triggers dopamine-fed neurons the most, but it also makes us get attached to things we perceive ourselves as owning. Dopamine is therefore crucial to how we make our decisions and develop our reference points.

In the fourth chapter, we discussed the concept of probability weighting. Probability weighting refers to how we *perceive* probability, which is rarely accurate when it comes to what a numerical probability actually is. Thus our brains see less-likely outcomes as more likely than they are, middling outcomes as fundamentally uncertain, and more-likely outcomes as less likely to happen than they are. Since we use probabilities to judge outcomes and make decisions, awareness of probability weighting is extremely important to becoming a good decision-maker.

In Chapter 5, we talked about the economic meaning of risk and how it fits into our decision-making process. People often talk about risk like it's a bad thing, but here we discussed that it is actually more neutral. Furthermore, some people's brains are more averse to risk than others. People generally behave in risk-averse ways because they want to avoid loss, but in the case that the smaller risk actually leads to a loss, we will take the big risk. People are not consistent with how they perceive risk. However, with the invention of modern portfolio theory, risk in investment is now seen as aggregate, and this viewpoint seems to help with improving financial decision-making.

In the sixth chapter, a more detailed definition of comparison was explored as we discussed how our brains construct value and preferences. The brain assigns each choice we have in a decision a value, but this value is subjective. This means that it is relative to the other choices, and thus our options can have a large effect on the choices we make. This can be seen in the decoy effect, wherein a third option skews people's perceptions of value and their decision-making. However, we also discussed strategies for being conscious of how we construct value, which can help avoid scams and general bad decision-making.

In Chapter 7, we dove deep into the theory of bounded rationality, and how being aware of this will improve your decision-making. Bounded rationality is the theory that humans' rational behavior has limits because of the way our brains are wired. So, we can only work with the time, information, and processing power that we have. However, these limitations can be worked around thanks to the structure of the world around us, which helps give us context and guide us. We also discussed the concept of "satisficing," or your brain tricking you into a false compromise, and how to avoid this to get what you really want more often.

In the eighth and last chapter, we talked about how behavioral economics works in social settings, specifically in small groups and large crowds. In small groups or one-on-one, game theory gives a set of options for how people will behave, and how their behaviors will affect each other. Game theory has its own division of economics, but the simple way to think about it is that people will generally make the most self-interested choice, which generally leads to a mediocre result for all the players in the game. Collaboration games in mid-size groups, meanwhile, can force people to work together for the common good as a commonly interested party. In larger crowds, the wisdom of the crowd dictates that the correct decision, judgment, or answer lies in the middle of a crowd's guesses, and crowds are therefore generally good at making decisions. However, any one of these scenarios can be derailed by overconfidence in an error or an incorrect decision. The main takeaway from this chapter, then, is the importance of thinking critically and knowing how to use humans' social behavior to one's best advantage when making decisions.

Behavioral economics is an exciting and rapidly growing field. With the understanding you've found in this book, you can now go out into the world more confident in your decision-making process (although not *too* confident!), and be better able to work around the brain's biases and cognitive quirks. If you consciously think about how your brain works to make decisions after you've finished this book, you've read it correctly. This book is designed to be a tool that will ultimately lead to better decisions and more productivity, and help you lead a happier, better-decided, more well-reasoned life. Think about how you make decisions, and you will be much more likely to make better ones in the future.

Thank you for reading my book.

Steven

Reference

Ariely, Dan. Camron, Ziv. Focusing on the Forgone: How Value Can Appear So Different to Buyers and Sellers. JOURNAL OF CONSUMER RESEARCH, Inc. Vol. 27. 0093-5301/2001/2703-0006$03.00. 2000.

Anagol, Santosh and Balasubramaniam, Vimal and Ramadorai, Tarun, Endowment Effects in the Field: Evidence from India's IPO Lotteries. Available at SSRN: https://ssrn.com/abstract=2702555 or http://dx.doi.org/10.2139/ssrn.2702555. 2017.

Beggan, J. On the social nature of nonsocial perception: The mere ownership effect. Journal of Personality and Social Psychology. 62 (2): 229–237. doi:10.1037/0022-3514.62.2.229. 1992.

Berridge, Kent C.Wanting and Liking:
Observations from the Neuroscience and
Psychology Laboratory',Inquiry,52:4,378 — 398.
2009.
http://dx.doi.org/10.1080/00201740903087359

Bortolotti, Stefania; Devetag, Giovanna; Ortmann,
Andreas. Group incentives or individual
incentives? A real-effort weak-link experiment.
Journal of Economic Psychology. 56 (C): 60–73.
ISSN 0167-4870. 2016.

Camerer, Colin. Progress in behavioral game
theory. Journal of Economic Perspectives. 11 (4):
172. doi:10.1257/jep.11.4.167. 1997.

Chen, James. Modern Portfolio Theory.
Investopedia. 2019.
https://www.investopedia.com/terms/m/modernpo
rtfoliotheory.asp

Crosetto, Paolo; Gaudeul, Alexia . A monetary measure of the strength and robustness of the attraction effect. Economics Letters. 149: 38–43. doi:10.1016/j.econlet.2016.09.031. ISSN 0165-1765. 2016.

Driver-Dunckley, Samanta J, Stacy M. Pathological gambling associated with dopamine agonist therapy in Parkinson's disease. Neurology.61(3):422-3. 10.1212/01.wnl.0000076478.45005.ec. 2003.

Esgate, Anthony; Groome, David. An Introduction to Applied Cognitive Psychology. Psychology Press. p. 201. ISBN 978-1-84169-318-7. 2005.

Feller, William. An Introduction to Probability Theory and Its Applications, (Vol 1), 3rd Ed. Wiley, ISBN 0-471-25708-7. 1968.

Gal, David. A psychological law of inertia and the illusion of loss aversion. Judgment and Decision Making. 1. 23-32. 2006.

Ganti, Akhilesh. Rational Choice Theory. Investopedia. 2019.
https://www.investopedia.com/terms/r/rational-choice-theory.asp

Galton, Francis. Vox Populi. Nature. DOI: https://doi.org/10.1038/075450a0. 1907.

Gigerenzer, Gerd; Selten, Reinhard. Bounded Rationality: The Adaptive Toolbox. MIT Press. ISBN 978-0-262-57164-7. 2002.

Glimcher Paul W. Understanding dopamine and reinforcement learning: The dopamine reward prediction error hypothesis. Proceedings of the National Academy of Sciences. 108 (Supplement 3) 15647-15654; DOI: 10.1073/pnas.1014269108. 2011.

https://www.pnas.org/content/108/Supplement_3/
15647

Hillson, David. Ruth Murray-Webster.
Understanding and Managing Risk Attitude.
Gower Publishing, Ltd. ISBN 978-0-566-08798-1.
2007.

How to get your own way? Compromise effect.
How to get your own way? 2019.
http://www.howtogetyourownway.com/effects/co
mpromise_effect.html

Kahneman, D. & Tversky, A. Advances in
prospect theory: Cumulative representation of
uncertainty. Journal of Risk and Uncertainty. 5
(4): 297–323. CiteSeerX 10.1.1.320.8769.
doi:10.1007/BF00122574. 1992.

Kahneman, Daniel; Tversky, Amos. Prospect Theory: An Analysis of Decision under Risk". Econometrica. 47 (2): 263–91. CiteSeerX 10.1.1.407.1910. doi:10.2307/1914185. JSTOR 1914185. 1979.

Kenton, Will. Behavioral Economics. Investopedia. 2019. https://www.investopedia.com/terms/b/behavioral economics.asp

Orr H. A. Fitness and its role in evolutionary genetics. Nature reviews. Genetics, 10(8), 531–539. doi:10.1038/nrg2603. 2009.

Plassmann, Hilke. John O'Doherty, Antonio Rangel. Orbitofrontal Cortex Encodes Willingness to Pay in Everyday Economic Transactions. Journal of Neuroscience. 27 (37) 9984-9988; DOI: 10.1523/JNEUROSCI.2131-07.2007

Rabin, Matthew. Incorporating fairness into game theory and economics. The American economic review, 1281-1302. 1993.

Rabin, Matthew. Risk Aversion and Expected-Utility Theory: A Calibration Theorem. Econometrica. 68 (5): 1281–1292. CiteSeerX 10.1.1.295.4269. doi:10.1111/1468-0262.00158. 2000.

Santangelo, Gabriella. Baronec, Paolo.Trojan, Luigi. Vitale, Carmine. Pathological gambling in Parkinson's disease. A comprehensive review. Volume 19, Issue 7, July 2013, Pages 645-653. https://doi.org/10.1016/j.parkreldis.2013.02.007

Schultz W. Neuronal Reward and Decision Signals: From Theories to Data. Physiological reviews, 95(3), 853–951. doi:10.1152/physrev.00023.2014. 2015.

Simon, Herbert A. A Behavioral Model of Rational Choice. The Quarterly Journal of Economics, Vol. 69, No. 1. pp. 99-118. The MIT Press. http://www.jstor.org/stable/1884852. 1955.

The Krazy Coupon Lady. Apple Back-to-School 2019: How to Score Cheap Computers & Tech. The Krazy Coupon Lady. 2019. https://thekrazycouponlady.com/tips/store-hacks/apple-back-to-school

Tversky, A.; Kahneman, D. Loss Aversion in Riskless Choice: A Reference Dependent Model. Quarterly Journal of Economics 106 (4): 1039–1061.1991.

Endnotes

---

[i] Kenton, Will. Behavioral Economics. Investopedia. 2019. https://www.investopedia.com/terms/b/behavioral economics.asp

[ii] Ganti, Akhilesh. Rational Choice Theory. Investopedia. 2019. https://www.investopedia.com/terms/r/rational-choice-theory.asp

[iii] Gigerenzer, Gerd; Selten, Reinhard. Bounded Rationality: The Adaptive Toolbox. MIT Press. ISBN 978-0-262-57164-7. 2002.

[iv] The Krazy Coupon Lady. Apple Back-to-School 2019: How to Score Cheap Computers & Tech. The Krazy Coupon Lady. 2019. https://thekrazycouponlady.com/tips/store-hacks/apple-back-to-school

[v] Kahneman, Daniel; Tversky, Amos. Prospect Theory: An Analysis of Decision under Risk". Econometrica. 47 (2): 263–91. CiteSeerX 10.1.1.407.1910. doi:10.2307/1914185. JSTOR 1914185. 1979.

[vi] Orr H. A. Fitness and its role in evolutionary genetics. Nature reviews. Genetics, 10(8), 531–539. doi:10.1038/nrg2603. 2009.

[vii] Glimcher Paul W. Understanding dopamine and reinforcement learning: The dopamine reward prediction error hypothesis. Proceedings of the National Academy of Sciences. 108 (Supplement 3) 15647-15654; DOI: 10.1073/pnas.1014269108. 2011.

https://www.pnas.org/content/108/Supplement_3/15647

[viii] Schultz W. Neuronal Reward and Decision Signals: From Theories to Data. Physiological

reviews, 95(3), 853–951.

doi:10.1152/physrev.00023.2014. 2015.

[ix] Berridge, Kent C.Wanting and Liking:

Observations from the Neuroscience and

Psychology Laboratory',Inquiry,52:4,378 — 398.

2009.

http://dx.doi.org/10.1080/00201740903087359

[x] Santangelo, Gabriella. Baronec, Paolo.Trojan,

Luigi. Vitale, Carmine. Pathological gambling in

Parkinson's disease. A comprehensive review.

Volume 19, Issue 7, July 2013, Pages 645-653.

https://doi.org/10.1016/j.parkreldis.2013.02.007

[xi] Driver-Dunckley, Samanta J, Stacy M.

Pathological gambling associated with dopamine

agonist therapy in Parkinson's disease.

Neurology.61(3):422-3.

10.1212/01.wnl.0000076478.45005.ec. 2003.

[xii] Kahneman, Daniel; Tversky, Amos. Prospect

Theory: An Analysis of Decision under Risk".

Econometrica. 47 (2): 263–91. CiteSeerX

10.1.1.407.1910. doi:10.2307/1914185. JSTOR
1914185. 1979.

[xiii] Beggan, J. On the social nature of nonsocial
perception: The mere ownership effect. Journal of
Personality and Social Psychology. 62 (2): 229–
237. doi:10.1037/0022-3514.62.2.229. 1992.

[xiv] Kahneman, D. & Tversky, A. Advances in
prospect theory: Cumulative representation of
uncertainty. Journal of Risk and Uncertainty. 5 (4):
297–323. CiteSeerX 10.1.1.320.8769.
doi:10.1007/BF00122574. 1992.

[xv] Anagol, Santosh and Balasubramaniam, Vimal
and Ramadorai, Tarun, Endowment Effects in the
Field: Evidence from India's IPO Lotteries.
Available at SSRN:
https://ssrn.com/abstract=2702555 or
http://dx.doi.org/10.2139/ssrn.2702555. 2017.

[xvi] Ariely, Dan. Camron, Ziv. Focusing on the
Forgone: How Value Can Appear So Different to
Buyers and Sellers. JOURNAL OF CONSUMER

RESEARCH, Inc. Vol. 27. 0093-5301/2001/2703-0006$03.00. 2000.

[xvii] Gal, David. A psychological law of inertia and the illusion of loss aversion. Judgment and Decision Making. 1. 23-32. 2006.

[xviii] Tversky, A.; Kahneman, D. Loss Aversion in Riskless Choice: A Reference Dependent Model. Quarterly Journal of Economics 106 (4): 1039–1061.1991.

[xix] Feller, William. An Introduction to Probability Theory and Its Applications, (Vol 1), 3rd Ed. Wiley, ISBN 0-471-25708-7. 1968.

[xx] Esgate, Anthony; Groome, David. An Introduction to Applied Cognitive Psychology. Psychology Press. p. 201. ISBN 978-1-84169-318-7. 2005.

[xxi] Hillson, David. Ruth Murray-Webster. Understanding and Managing Risk Attitude.

Gower Publishing, Ltd. ISBN 978-0-566-08798-1. 2007.

[xxii] Rabin, Matthew. Risk Aversion and Expected-Utility Theory: A Calibration Theorem. Econometrica. 68 (5): 1281–1292. CiteSeerX 10.1.1.295.4269. doi:10.1111/1468-0262.00158. 2000.

[xxiii] Chen, James. Modern Portfolio Theory. Investopedia. 2019. https://www.investopedia.com/terms/m/modern portfoliotheory.asp

[xxiv] Crosetto, Paolo; Gaudeul, Alexia . A monetary measure of the strength and robustness of the attraction effect. Economics Letters. 149: 38–43. doi:10.1016/j.econlet.2016.09.031. ISSN 0165-1765. 2016.

[xxv] How to get your own way? Compromise effect. How to get your own way? 2019.

http://www.howtogetyourownway.com/effects/compromise_effect.html

[xxvi] Plassmann, Hilke. John O'Doherty, Antonio Rangel. Orbitofrontal Cortex Encodes Willingness to Pay in Everyday Economic Transactions. Journal of Neuroscience. 27 (37) 9984-9988; DOI: 10.1523/JNEUROSCI.2131-07.2007

[xxvii] Gigerenzer, Gerd; Selten, Reinhard. Bounded Rationality: The Adaptive Toolbox. MIT Press. ISBN 978-0-262-57164-7. 2002.

[xxviii] Simon, Herbert A. A Behavioral Model of Rational Choice. The Quarterly Journal of Economics, Vol. 69, No. 1. pp. 99-118. The MIT Press. http://www.jstor.org/stable/1884852. 1955.

[xxix] Camerer, Colin. Progress in behavioral game theory. Journal of Economic Perspectives. 11 (4): 172. doi:10.1257/jep.11.4.167. 1997.

[xxx] Rabin, M. Incorporating fairness into game theory and economics. The American economic review, 1281-1302. 1993.

[xxxi] Bortolotti, Stefania; Devetag, Giovanna; Ortmann, Andreas. Group incentives or individual incentives? A real-effort weak-link experiment. Journal of Economic Psychology. 56 (C): 60–73. ISSN 0167-4870. 2016.

[xxxii] Galton, Francis. Vox Populi. Nature. DOI: https://doi.org/10.1038/075450a0. 1907.

Lightning Source UK Ltd.
Milton Keynes UK
UKHW010258090223
416650UK00003B/855